MARVELLOUS BLACK INVENTORS

written by
Joy James

illustrated by
Karen Dowie

Michael Terence Publishing

— For Milton, Jade and Jules —

INTRODUCING OUR MARVELLOUS BLACK INVENTORS...

STEVE HENSEN..2

CLARENCE ELDER..4

WILLIAM LANE...6

NATHANIEL ALEXANDER..8

THOMAS LECKY...10

YOUMNA MOUHAMAD...12

DAVID PHILLIPS and CHARLES JACKSON...14

WINSTON SIMON...16

LANNY SMOOT...18

WILLIAM HARWELL...20

ROSETTA THARPE..22

RICHARD TURERE...24

GLADYS WEST..26

HERMAN GRIMES..28

DONNA AUGUSTE..30

BENJAMIN MONTGOMERY...32

STEVE HENSEN

Do you eat your vegetables?

They are good for you and are often called greens even though they come in many different colours!

Steve was a cook who noticed that some people didn't like to eat their greens, so he made a delicious sauce to put on top and they ate up all their greens!
He called it ranch dressing.

What other colours are some vegetables?

CLARENCE ELDER

Do you help to save energy in your house?

Clarence invented a system to help save energy in homes and offices and other buildings. He called it an occustat and it turns off lights and heaters when no one is there.

Have you seen the lights turn on when you enter a room? It's like magic!

Can you think of other ways to save energy?

WILLIAM LANE

Do you like to dance?

William invented tap dancing and wore special shoes that made lots of noisy, tapping sounds when he tap danced!

He loved all types of dancing and was known as 'Master Juba – King of All Dancers'.

Can you dance the waltz or ballet or hip hop?

NATHANIEL ALEXANDER

Do you have folding chairs at home or school?

Nathaniel invented these chairs to help save space when they are not being used.

You can pack them away or take them out to use in the garden for barbecues or in the park for picnics or in a big hall for all types of events — very useful!

Do you like barbecues or picnics or parties?

THOMAS LECKY

Where would you find a cow?

They give us milk to drink. You can also use milk to make cheese and yoghurt and ice cream and lots of other lovely food!

Thomas lived in Jamaica in the Caribbean where he bred two special types of cows, called Jamaica Red and Jamaica Black. They liked living in a hot country and made lots of delicious milk!

Can you think of other types of milk?

YOUMNA MOUHAMAD

Does your hair sometimes get into a tangle?

Youmna had lots of lovely, curly hair which was sometimes painful to comb through – ouch!

She wanted an easier way to untangle her hair, so she made a comb which helped to easily undo her tangles.

She called her comb the deluxe detangler — great name!

Do you like trying different hairstyles?

DAVID PHILLIPS and CHARLES JACKSON

What are citrus fruits?

These are oranges and lemons and grapefruit.
They are juicy and taste tangy.

Did you know that there are many types of oranges?

David and Charles used tangerines and mandarin oranges
to make the ortanique fruit — what a fancy name!
It was very juicy and sweet - yum!

Can you think of any other orange coloured food?

WINSTON SIMON

Have you played on a drum? Boom, boom, boom!

Winston made a drum out of metal which was called
a ping pong steel pan.

He could play many different musical notes on it and
made beautiful tunes that people loved to hear.
He played his steel pan at the
Trinidad and Tobago carnival in the Caribbean.

What musical instrument do you like to play?

LANNY SMOOT

Do you like watching cartoons?

Lanny could make imaginary things like cartoons look like real life. This is called special effects!

He worked at Disneyland and used lights and technology to make amazing, magical special effects!

Can you think of any films that use special effects?

WILLIAM HARWELL

Do you look for stars in the sky at night-time?

They might be satellites instead! These are machines that are sent up into space to collect information about Earth and other planets but sometimes they might get lost!

William built a machine with a long magnetic arm to help get them back by stretching out and grabbing them — wonderful!

Can you think of other things that work this way?

ROSETTA THARPE

Do you like to listen to music?

There are lots of different types of music,
such as jazz or reggae or pop music.

Rosetta played the electric guitar and mixed gospel music with rhythm and blues. She played loud, strong beats using a new technique and invented rock and roll music! She was known as the Godmother of rock and roll!

What type of music do you like?

RICHARD TURERE

Do you live near a farm or woodland with animals?

Imagine living near lions and other wild animals!

Richard is a Maasai herder living in Kenya in Africa who needed to find a way to protect his farm animals from lions! He built a flashing light system called Lion Lights which helped to keep lions away from his animal enclosures.

What animals would you like to see close up?

GLADYS WEST

Do you know what GPS stands for?

It's the Global Positioning System which helps us to find places that we want to travel to and visit.

Gladys invented GPS! She was very good at doing maths and spent a lot of time measuring distances between all the different places on Earth to help make maps of towns and cities — brilliant!

Can you draw a map of your neighbourhood?

HERMAN GRIMES

Have you flown in an aeroplane?

They have big wings to help them fly.

Herman built an aeroplane with wings that could be folded up to make it smaller! These aeroplanes were used in World War II as they were small enough to fit on to army ships and into small hangars where planes are kept.

What else has wings and can fly?

DONNA AUGUSTE

Have you used a computer or laptop?

It's easier to hold a smaller machine!

Donna worked for Apple Computers and used new technology to make computer programmes for a smaller handheld machine that worked like smartphones or tablets.

Do you know what people used before we had these machines?

BENJAMIN MONTGOMERY

Have you been on a boat or ferry or yacht?

In the old days, steamboats were used and they sometimes got stuck in shallow rivers, so Benjamin built a special propeller which helped them to move easily in shallow water. These steamboats carried people and deliveries to different places.

Do you know any nursery rhymes?

Here is one about boats:

Row, row, row your boat, gently down the stream
Merrily, merrily, merrily, merrily,
life is but a dream!

Acknowledgements

A huge thank you to Karen Dowie for her creative ideas and lovely illustrations.

Grateful thanks to Keith Abbott at Michael Terence Publishing for his advice and help in getting this book published.

Lots of love and thanks to my wonderful family for inspiring and encouraging me on my writing journey.

About the Author

Joy James lives in London with her family. She works at a university and writes non-fiction children's books to help educate and inform curious, young minds.

Her Black Inventors series includes *101 Black Inventors and their Inventions* and *Another 101 Black Inventions and their Inventions* which are aimed at upper primary and lower secondary school ages.

Other books in the series in this age group include *Brilliant Black Inventors* and *Amazing Black Inventors*.

First published in paperback in 2023 by Michael Terence Publishing
www.mtp.agency

ISBN 9781800946408

Copyright © 2023 Joy James

Joy James has asserted the right to be identified as the author of this work in accordance with the Copyright, Designs and Patents Act 1988

No part of this publication may be reproduced, stored in a retrieval system, or transmitted in any form or by any means, electronic, mechanical, photocopying, recording or otherwise, without the prior permission of the publisher

Illustrated by Karen Dowie